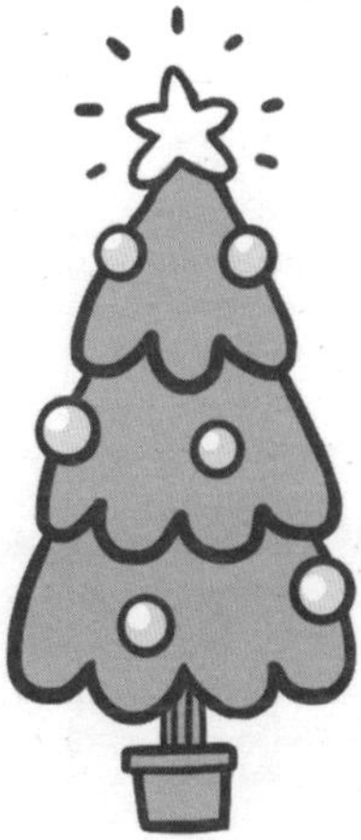

**Written by Caroline Rowlands.**
**Illustrations by Steve James.**
**Cover artwork based on designs by Thy Bui.**

First published in Great Britain in 2025 by Red Shed, part of Farshore

An imprint of HarperCollins*Publishers*
1 London Bridge Street, London SE1 9GF
www.farshore.co.uk

HarperCollins*Publishers*
Macken House, 39/40 Mayor Street Upper,
Dublin 1, D01 C9W8, Ireland

Red Shed is a registered trademark of HarperCollins*Publishers* Ltd.



ISBN 978 0 00 873919 5
Printed and bound in Great Britain by Clays Ltd, Elcograf S.p.A.
001

A CIP catalogue record for this title is available from the British Library.

# AMAZING PUZZLES & QUIZZES

# CHRISTMAS

RED SHED

**Have fun cracking clues, solving puzzles and tackling quizzes in this festive book.**

**You'll find loads of amazing activities and exciting brain teasers to challenge yourself with – or you can test your friends and family for hours of fun together!**

Along the way, you'll find a mix of all sorts of puzzles – spot the difference, missing letters, quizzes, mazes and more. Each puzzle has instructions at the top of the page that tell you what you need to do. Once you've got your answer, or if you get stuck, head to the back of the book to check the solution.

**Guaranteed to get you feeling Christmassy . . . enjoy the festive fun!**

# Spot the Pair: Which Elf?

Only one of the labelled images on this page is identical to this little elf – the rest have small differences.

Can you work out which elf is an exact match?

a) 

b) 

c) 

d) 

Answers on page 77

# Spot the Difference: Santa's Workshop

Answers on page 77

There are eight differences to spot between these two scenes. Can you find them all?

Answers on page 77

## Festive Fun Quiz

1. **Where do children send their Christmas wish lists to?**

**a)** The North Pole
**b)** The South Pole
**c)** The Moon

2. **What vehicle does Santa use to deliver presents on Christmas Eve?**

**a)** A submarine
**b)** A spaceship
**c)** A sleigh

3. **Which animals help Santa with his deliveries?**

**a)** Elephants
**b)** Reindeer
**c)** Donkeys

Answers on page 78

## How Many Presents?

Can you help this little elf count
up all the presents below?

Answers on page 78

## Gift Wrapped

Each of the presents below has a different wrapping paper pattern. Can you work out which ribbon on the opposite page matches each present?

1.

2.

3.

4.

5.



Answers on page 78

a)

b)

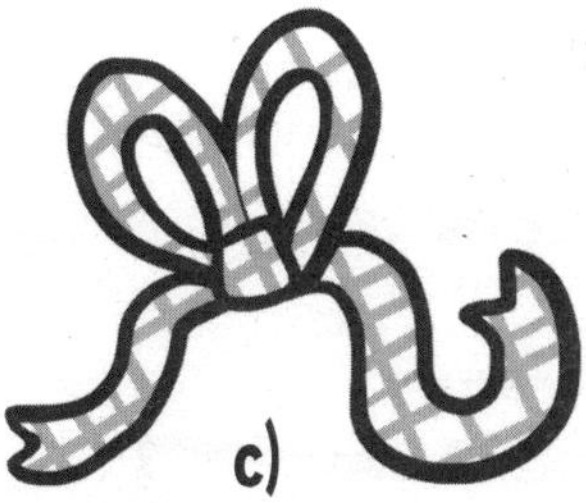

c)

d)

e)

Answers on page 78

## Christmas Traditions Quiz

**1. Which sweet treat is often found in an Advent Calendar?**

**a)** Ice cream
**b)** Chocolate
**c)** Candyfloss

**2. What clothing item is usually left out on Christmas Eve, to be filled with presents?**

**a)** A stocking or sock
**b)** A pair of pants
**c)** A woolly hat

**3. Which of these is traditionally eaten for Christmas dinner?**

**a)** An owl
**b)** A pigeon
**c)** A turkey



Answers on page 79

# North Pole Maze

Can you help Rudolph find his way through the snow to reach his friend?

Answers on page 79

# Broken Bots

This naughty elf keeps pushing toy robots off the shelf. Can you fix these three broken robots by pairing up the pieces that fit together exactly? Every numbered broken fragment fits with exactly one lettered fragment. The robots should all look like the one on the shelf.

1) 

2) 

3) 

a) 

b) 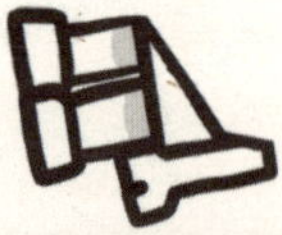

c) 

Answers on page 80

# Super Snowman Quiz

**1. What is a snowman made of?**

**a)** Frozen peas
**b)** Frozen water
**c)** Frozen jelly

**2. Which vegetable is often used to create a snowman's nose?**

**a)** A potato
**b)** A cabbage
**c)** A carrot

**3. No two snowflakes are the same. True or false?**

**4. Which item completes this song title? *Jingle* ________.**

**a)** Bills
**b)** Bells
**c)** Bulls

Answers on page 80

# Emotion Match

Each of the sentences below describes the emotions shown on exactly one of the snowmen. Can you match them up?

a) 

b) 

c) 

d) 

e) 

1. I'm feeling happy because I love Christmas.
2. I'm feeling sad because Christmas is over.
3. I'm feeling sleepy because I was up so early.
4. It's Christmas – I'm feeling ready to party!
5. I'm feeling scared. What if I'm on the naughty list?



Answers on page 80

# Northern Delights Quiz

## 1. Which country is the North Pole in?

**a)** Iceland
**b)** Finland
**c)** It is not in a country

## 2. Which imaginary lines on a map run between the North Pole and South Pole?

**a)** The equator (halfway between the North Pole and South Pole)
**b)** Lines of longitude (that circle the globe vertically)
**c)** Lines of latitude (that circle the globe parallel to the equator)

## 3. During the summer in the North Pole, the sun shines all day and night long. True or false?

Answers on page 80

# Christmas Riddles

Can you work out the answers
to these five riddles?

**1.** When does Christmas come before Halloween?

**2.** I have lots of needles but
cannot sew. What am I?

**3.** I come from the sky but I am colder than
rain. No two pieces are the same. What am I?

**4.** When there's snow, I go faster. What am I?

**5.** I'm tall when I'm young but short
when I'm old. What am I?

**Answers on page 80**

# Follow the Line: Christmas Lights Tangle

Oops! These elves have got their lights all tangled up. Can you work out which lights belong to which Christmas tree?

Answers on page 81

## Hidden Words I

Some words have other words hidden within them – for example, the word 'IS' is hiding in the word 'CHRISTMAS'. Each of the words below has a word hiding inside it. Can you find them all? Clues are given to help you.

**1.** STOCKING

**Clue:** A royal ruler.

**2.** MISTLETOE

**Clue:** A part of your foot.

**3.** GINGERBREAD

**Clue:** What you do with a book.

**4.** REINDEER

**Clue:** The opposite to out.

**5.** DECORATIONS

**Clue:** A rodent.



Answers on page 81

# Chimney Maze

Can you help Santa find his way down the chimney so he can deliver the presents?

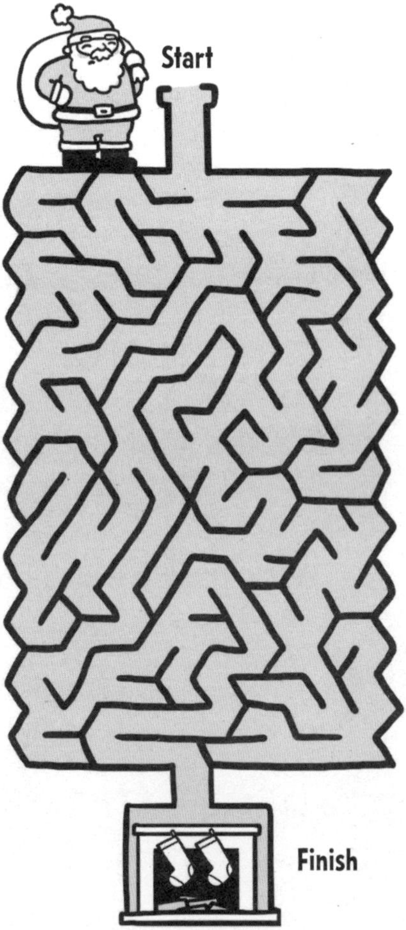


Answers on page 81

# Whose Hat?

Oops! These elves have muddled up their hats. Can you pair each elf with the hat that matches their outfit?

1. 

2. 

3. 

4. 

5. 

Answers on page 82

Can you spot a hat that doesn't belong to anyone?

a)

b)

c)

d)

e)

f)

Answers on page 82

# Spot the Difference: Santa's Sleigh

Answers on page 82

There are eight differences to spot between these two images. Can you find them all?

Answers on page 82

# Spot the Pair: Smiley Santa

Only one of the labelled images on this page is identical to Santa – the rest have small differences.

Can you work out which image is an exact match?

a)

b)

c)

d)

Answers on page 83

# Missing Letters: Festive Treats

In each of the sentences below is a word that is missing some letters. Can you work out what the five words are? Each word is spelled out in capital letters.

Many people enjoy watching a M_VIE at Christmas.

A G_NG_R_READ house is baked in an oven.

PR_SE_TS are lovely to receive and even better to give.

You can build a S_OW_AN when there is lots of snow.

Candy C_NES taste delicious, especially at Christmas.

Answers on page 83

## Missing Words: Merry Christmas

Each of the sentences on the opposite page is missing a word. Can you select the one correct word from the list below to complete each of the seven sentences? There is one word that does NOT fit in any of the sentences – can you work out which one it is?

**Pudding**
**List**
**Paper**
**Advent**
**Decorate**
**Cards**
**Elf**
**Wreath**

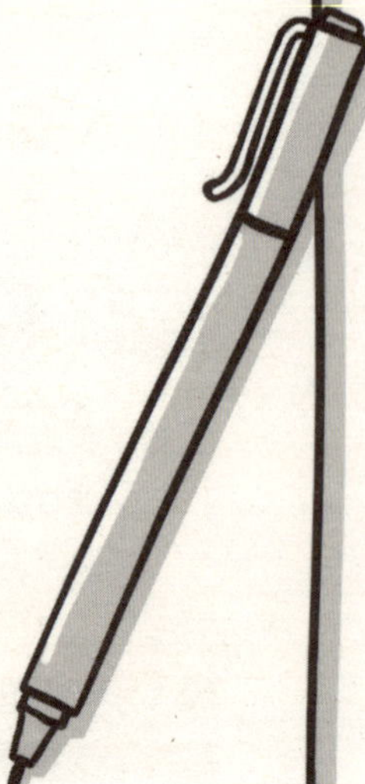


Answers on page 83

1. Wrapping ________ comes in lots of colours and patterns and is used to wrap gifts.

2. People send and receive Christmas ________.

3. You might write a ________ of all the presents you want from Santa at Christmas.

4. It is traditional to ________ a Christmas tree.

5. Some people also have the tradition of putting an ________ on a shelf.

6. In December, some people count down to Christmas by opening a door on an ________ calendar every day.

7. Some people decorate their front door with a Christmas ________.

Answers on page 83

## Reorder Puzzle: Santa

Santa is looking a little mixed up! Can you work out the correct letter order (reading from top to bottom) that would show the complete image?

a)

b)

c)

d)

e)

f)

Answers on page 84

# Super Snow Quiz

## 1. How many points does a snowflake usually have?

**a)** Two
**b)** Six
**c)** Ten

## 2. What is a snowflake made of?

**a)** Ice crystals
**b)** Dust particles
**c)** Mashed potato

## 3. According to NASA, there may be snow on Mars. True or false?

## 4. What is the word for a rapid movement of snow down a slope?

**a)** A hurricane
**b)** An avalanche
**c)** A tornado

Answers on page 84

## Santa's Songs Quiz

Which line comes next in these seasonal songs?

**1. Deck the halls with . . .**

**a)** boughs of ivy
**b)** boughs of holly
**c)** boughs of daffodils

**2. Dashing through the snow . . .**

**a)** on a motorbike on Tuesday
**b)** on a camel eating hay
**c)** on a one-horse open sleigh

**3. On the first day of Christmas, my true love sent to me . . .**

**a)** a pigeon in an apple tree
**b)** a partridge in a pear tree
**c)** a parrot in a lemon tree

Answers on page 84

# Follow the Line: Reindeer Tangle

These reindeer reins are in a tangle! Can you follow the lines to work out which elf has which reindeer?

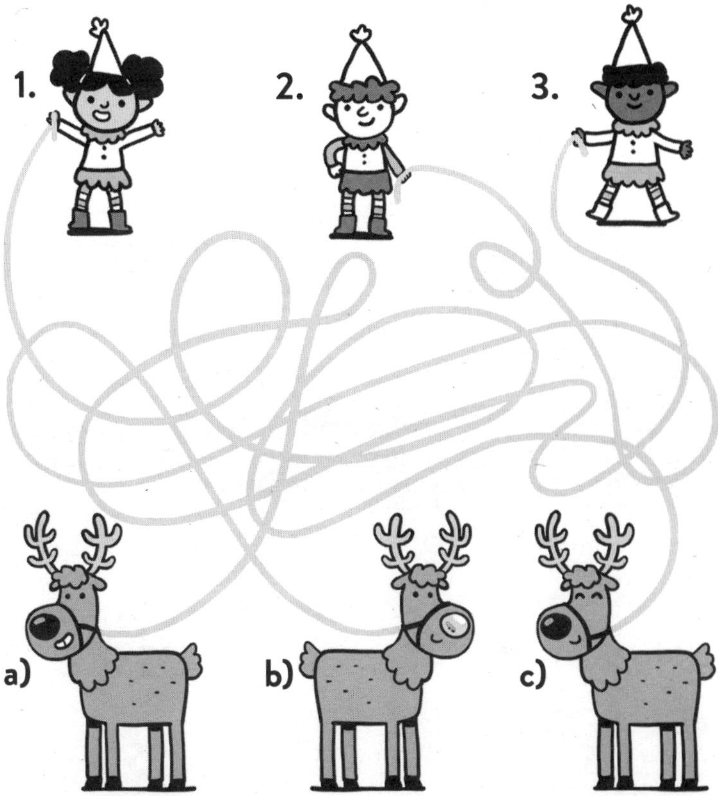


Answers on page 84

# Jigsaw: Sleigh Ride

A piece is missing from this jigsaw! Can you work out which of the puzzle pieces below fits exactly into the empty space on the opposite page to complete the image?

a) 

b) 

c) 

d) 

e) 

Answers on page 85

Answers on page 85

## Christmas Around the World Quiz

1. **In Ukraine, which decoration do most people have on their tree?**

**a)** A spider's web
**b)** A bird's nest
**c)** A frog's lily pad

2. **In Great Britain, what was traditionally placed in a Christmas pudding and thought to bring good luck to the person who finds it?**

**a)** A spoon
**b)** A coin
**c)** A boiled egg

3. **Which of these foods is a popular meal choice for families in Japan on Christmas Eve?**

**a)** French fries
**b)** Hamburgers
**c)** Fried chicken



Answers on page 85

# Reorder Puzzle: Rudolph

Oh *deer*, Ruldolph is looking a little mixed up! Can you work out the correct letter order (reading from left to right) that would show the complete image?

a) b) c) d) e)

Answers on page 85

# Christmas Tree Maze

Can you help the Christmas fairy find her way through the Christmas tree to reach the top?

Answers on page 86

# Christmas Garden Quiz

**1. Which prickly plant is linked with Christmas?**

**a)** Holly
**b)** Cactus
**c)** Rose

**2. Which plant is it traditional to kiss under at Christmas time?**

**a)** Ivy
**b)** Mistletoe
**c)** Tulip

**3. Which type of tree is the traditional Christmas tree?**

**a)** A palm tree
**b)** A fir tree
**c)** An oak tree

Answers on page 86

# Christmas Tree Shadows

Can you match each Christmas tree to its shadow on the opposite page?

1.

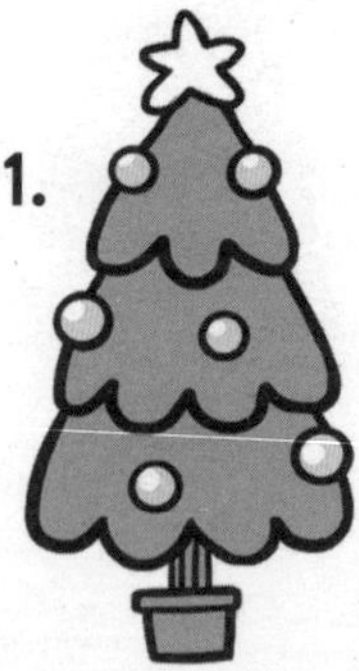

2.

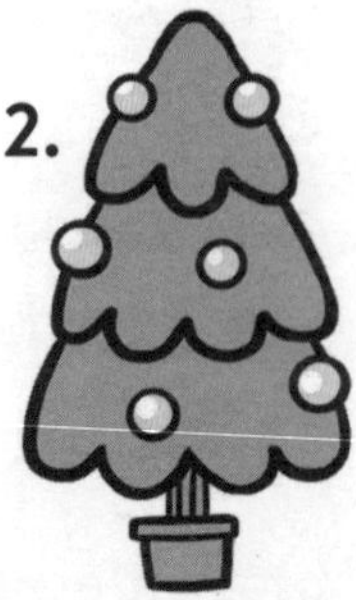

3.

4.

5.

Answers on page 87

a)

b)

c)

d)

e)

Answers on page 87

## Snowflake Spotter

These snowflakes are falling fast!
How many can you count in the image below?

Answers on page 87

# Missing Letters: Christmas Recipes

These **words from a Christmas recipe book** are missing some letters. Can you fill in the gaps to reveal the delicious festive foods?

T_R_EY

MI__E _IE_

CR_NB__RY SA_CE

CHRIS_MAS PUD_IN_

CHO_OL_TE

CHR_ST_AS C__E

R_AST P__ATOES

Answers on page 87

# Winter Sports Quiz

1. **How often do the Winter Olympic and Paralympic Games take place?**

**a)** Once a year
**b)** Every two years
**c)** Every four years

2. **Which of these is NOT a winter sport?**

**a)** Fencing
**b)** Ice hockey
**c)** Curling

3. **The world's longest sledging run, in Switzerland, is around 15km long. True or false?**

4. **Which of these sports was invented in 1965 and became a Winter Olympic sport in 1998?**

**a)** Skiing
**b)** Snowboarding
**c)** Skating

Answers on page 88

# Missing Letters: Santa's Clothes

All of Santa's clothes have either one, two or three letters missing from their labels. Can you work out the missing letters to complete the words?

**1.** H _ T

**2.** C _ A _

**3.** BE _ T

**4.** T _ OU _ ER _

**5.** B _ OT _

Answers on page 88

## Delivery Map

Can you work out the correct coordinates for the **presents** on Santa's delivery list below? To find the coordinates, trace a line from the gift down to the letter below it, then across to the number next to it – then put the letter and number together. The first coordinate is given as an example.

Example: Bike
**A2**

**1.** Rollerskates

**2.** Football

**3.** Robot



Answers on page 88

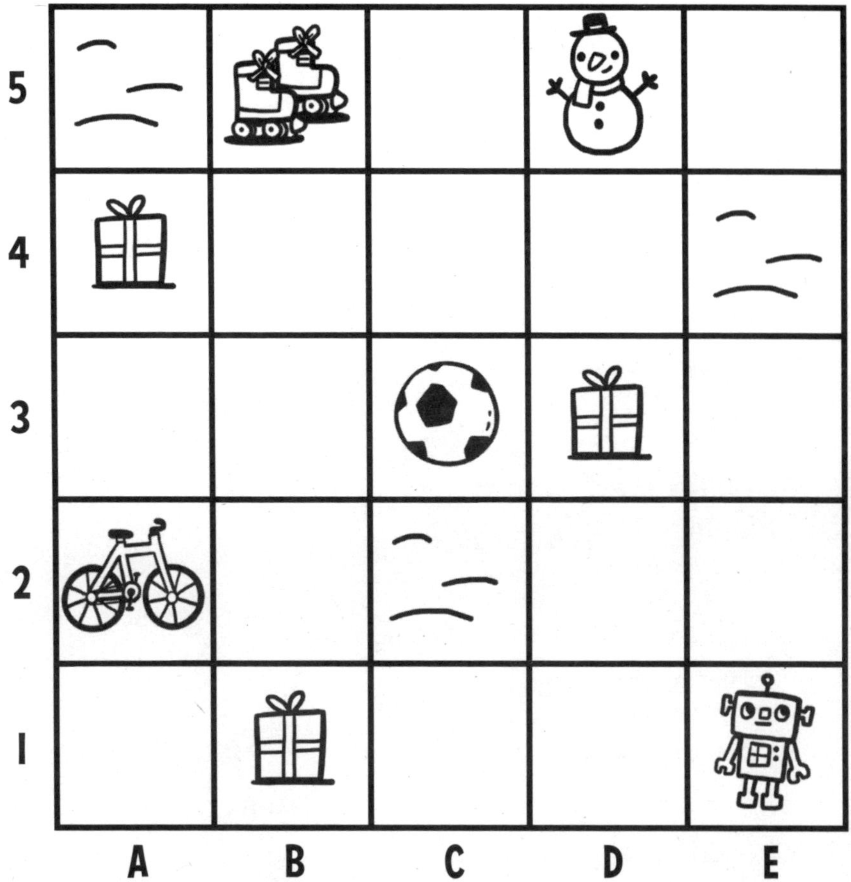


Answers on page 88

## 'Tis the Season Quiz

1. **Which of these items is NOT traditionally put on top of a Christmas tree?**

**a)** A fairy
**b)** A star
**c)** A rubber duck

2. **Which of these items would you NOT wrap around a Christmas tree?**

**a)** Tinsel
**b)** Sticky tape
**c)** Lights

3. **Which of these items would you find on a Christmas tree?**

**a)** A bauble
**b)** A puppy
**c)** A sausage

Answers on page 88

# Christmas Codebreaker

Below are the names of **four presents**, all disguised using an alphabet code, where each letter has been replaced with a number, as shown in the grid. Can you use the grid to crack the code and reveal the presents?

| A | B | C | D | E | F | G | H | I | J | K | L | M |
|---|---|---|---|---|---|---|---|---|---|---|---|---|
| 1 | 16 | 3 | 4 | 8 | 6 | 17 | 21 | 9 | 10 | 25 | 12 | 23 |

| N | O | P | Q | R | S | T | U | V | W | X | Y | Z |
|---|---|---|---|---|---|---|---|---|---|---|---|---|
| 14 | 15 | 11 | 20 | 13 | 26 | 18 | 2 | 22 | 5 | 24 | 7 | 19 |

**1.** 16 1 12 12

**2.** 16 9 25 8

**3.** 3 15 23 11 2 18 8 13

**4.** 11 8 14 3 9 12 3 1 26 8

Try making up your own code for someone to crack!

Answers on page 89

## Skating Fun Maze

Can you help this elf skate across the pond to find his friends?

Answers on page 89

## Icy Trivia Quiz

1. **At what temperature does water freeze and turn to ice?**

**a)** 100°C
**b)** 0°C
**c)** -100°C

2. **We are living through an Ice Age. The current Ice Age started around 2.6 million years ago. True or false?**

3. **Which of the animals below lives in an icy habitat?**

**a)** Elephant
**b)** Polar bear
**c)** Meerkat

Answers on page 90

## Spot the Difference: Snowpark Fun!

Answers on page 90

There are eight differences to spot between these two images. Can you find them all?

Answers on page 90

## Christmas Foods Quiz

**1. Which country serves cold fish as a first course for Christmas dinner?**

**a)** Sweden
**b)** Spain
**c)** Mexico

**2. In Puerto Rico, which meat is traditionally served for Christmas dinner?**

**a)** Roast beef
**b)** Roast chicken
**c)** Roast suckling pig

**3. In Germany, a gingerbread house is called a *pfefferkuchenhaus*. True or false?**

Answers on page 91

# Follow the Path: Christmas Market

Can you follow the pathways below to work out where each snowman is going?

**a)** Pond **b)** Market **c)** Tree **d)** North Pole

Answers on page 91

## Twelve Birds of Christmas Quiz

The 'Twelve Days of Christmas' is a traditional song that counts up the gifts the singer receives each day, from a single partridge to twelve drummers drumming.

**1. Where can you find the partridge?**

**a)** In a pear tree
**b)** In a bird cage
**c)** In the sky

**2. Which birds were a-laying eggs?**

**a)** Sparrows
**b)** Geese
**c)** Parrots

**3. Which of these birds are NOT mentioned in the carol?**

**a)** Swans
**b)** Calling birds
**c)** Ostriches



Answers on page 91

# Candy Cane Maze

Can you help this little elf find her way through the maze for a sweet treat?

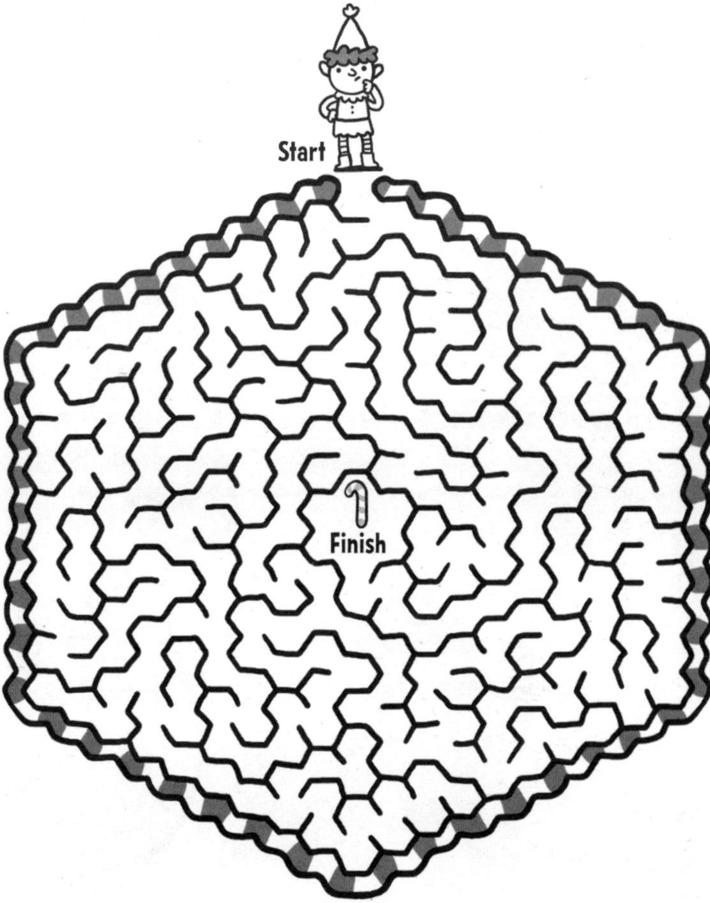


Answers on page 91 

# Spot the Pair: Gingerbread

Yum! The elves have been busy baking. Can you spot which gingerbread biscuit below is the same as this one?

a)

b)

c)

d)



Answers on page 92

# Secret Scribbler: Decoration Time

Someone has been up to no good and has scribbled out all the vowels (the letters A, E, I, O and U) from these **four Christmas decorations**. Can you work out what vowels are missing to identify them? A clue is given after each word to help you.

**1.** T ■ N S ■ L

**Clue:** Sparkly and shiny, you wrap it around your Christmas tree.

**2.** W R ■ ■ T H

**Clue:** Usually green and often on a front door.

**3.** F ■ ■ R Y

**Clue:** This takes pride of place on top of the tree.

**4.** L ■ G H T S

**Clue:** Guaranteed to make your Christmas tree stand out in the dark.

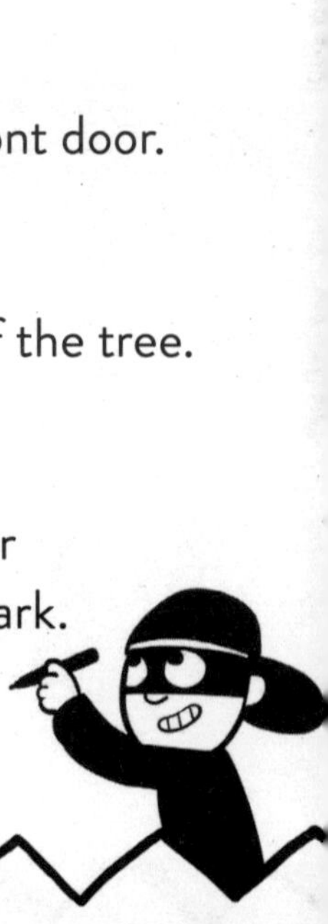

Answers on page 92

# Follow the Line: Tinsel Tangle

Can you follow the different tinsel strands to find out which one is decorating each tree?

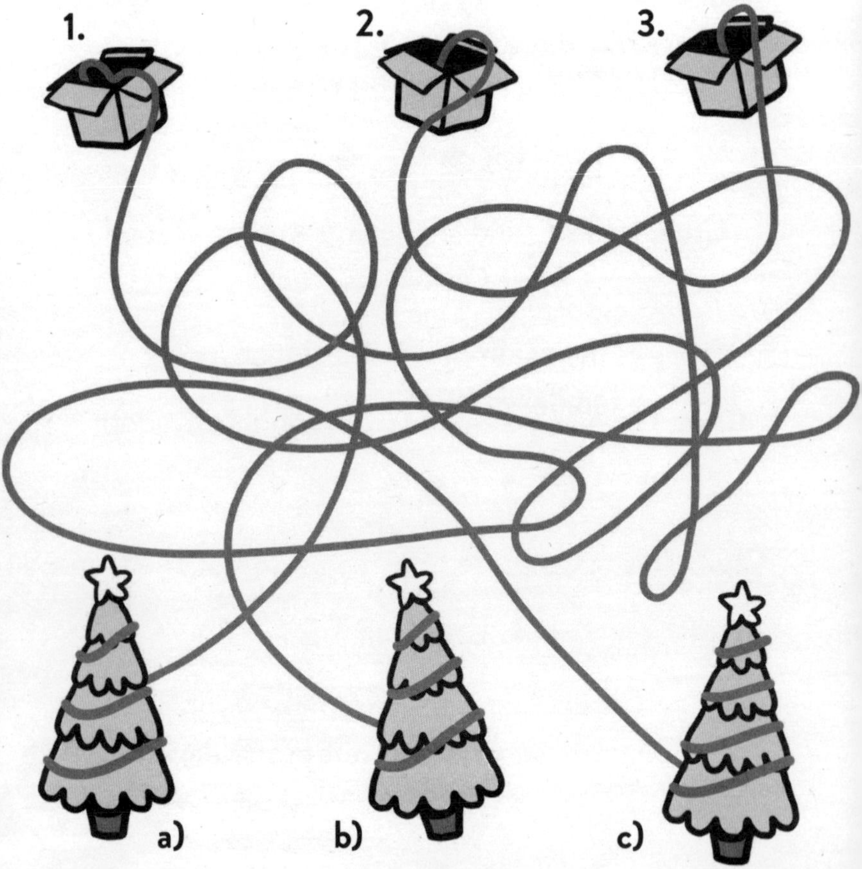




Answers on page 92

# Christmas Cake Quiz

**1. Which country enjoys a Christmas cake called *panettone*?**

**a)** Portugal
**b)** Italy
**c)** New Zealand

**2. The French enjoy eating a chocolate cake called *Buche de Noel* at Christmas time. True or false?**

**3. Which of the cakes below is enjoyed by German familes during Christmas?**

**a)** Red velvet cake
**b)** Stollen
**c)** Victoria sponge

Answers on page 92

## Christmas Treasure Hunt

You've found a treasure map! It includes a set of directions, starting at square A1 (labelled with an 'X'). Follow the path described in the instructions. What does the path lead to – the **present**, the **stocking**, the **gingerbread** or **Santa's sack**? Does the path cross anything else on the way there?

**Start** at A1

**Up** 2 squares

**Right** 1 square

**Down** 1 square

**Right** 2 squares

**Up** 3 squares



Answers on page 93

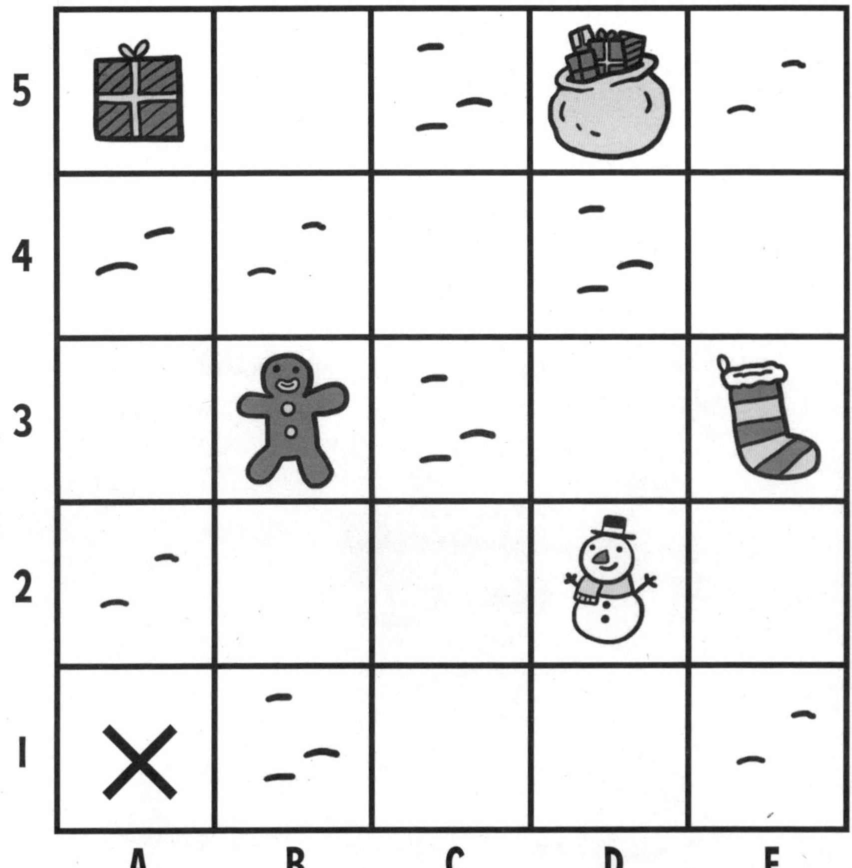


Answers on page 93

# Jigsaw: Santa's Tree

A piece is missing from this jigsaw! Can you work out which of the puzzle pieces below fits exactly into the empty space on the opposite page to complete the image?

a)

b)

c)

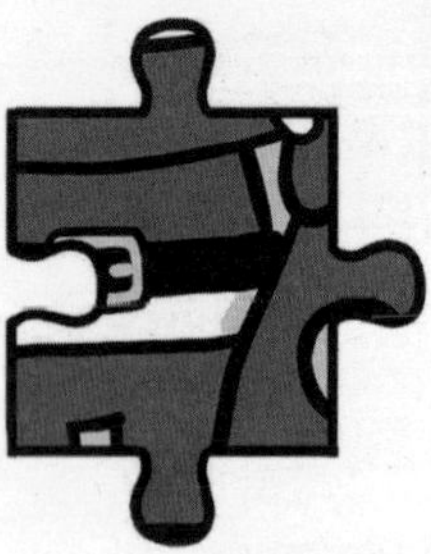

d)

e)



Answers on page 93

Answers on page 93

## Missing Words: Happy Christmas!

Each of the sentences on the opposite page is missing a word. Can you select the one correct word from the list below to complete each of the six sentences? There is one word that does NOT fit in any of the sentences – can you work out which one it is?

**Reindeer**
**Santa**
**Elf**
**Rudolph**
**Wreath**
**Stocking**
**Cracker**

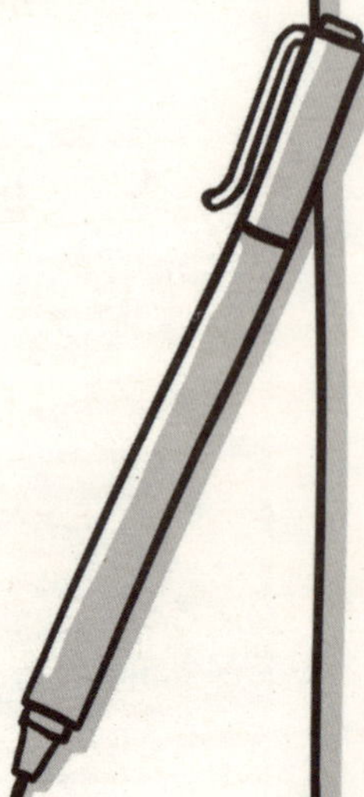



Answers on page 93

1. You pull a ________ before Christmas dinner and find a joke and hat inside.

2. A ________ has four legs and helps pull Santa's sleigh.

3. You might see ________'s red nose glowing on Christmas Eve.

4. A ________ often hangs on the front door.

5. Ho ho ho! The elves hear ________ say this a lot!

6. It's always fun to hang up a ________ on Christmas Eve, as in the morning it could be filled with lots and lots of presents!

Answers on page 93

## Secret Santa

Can you work out which elf has given which present, using the clues below?

**1.** This elf's present is square and wrapped in spotty paper with a bow.

**2.** This elf's present has a stripey wrapping paper and is the smallest.

**3.** This elf's present is round and wrapped in starry paper, and has a bow.

**4.** This elf's present is square and wrapped in spotty paper, but has no bow.



Answers on page 94

a)

b)

c)

d)

Answers on page 94

# Secret Scribbler: Winter Wonderland

Someone has been up to no good and has scribbled out all the vowels (the letters A, E, I, O and U) from these wintry words. Can you work out what vowels are missing to identify them? A clue is given after each word to help you.

**1.** C_NDY C_N_

**Clue:** A sweet treat with stripes.

**2.** IC_ SK_T_NG

**Clue:** A fun activity in winter.

**3.** SN_WM_N

**Clue:** Often has a scarf and carrot for a nose.

**4.** CH_C_L_T_

**Clue:** Often found behind the doors of an Advent calendar.

Answers on page 94

# Festive Riddles!

Can you guess the answers to these four riddles?

**1.** I can travel all over the world, just like Santa, without ever leaving my corner. What am I?

**2.** What is at the end of Christmas?

**3.** Which of Santa's reindeer can you see in space?

**4.** What bites but doesn't have teeth?

**Answers on page 94**

## Hidden Words II

Some words have other words hidden within them – for example, the word 'TO' is hiding in the word 'STOCKING'. Each of the words below has a word hiding inside it. Can you find them all? Clues are given to help you.

**1.** SPICE

**Clue:** Another word for frozen water.

**2.** DONKEY

**Clue:** Something that will unlock a door.

**3.** DOUGHNUT

**Clue:** Something a squirrel might eat.

**4.** SONG

**Clue:** The opposite to off.

**5.** GARLAND

**Clue:** The part of Earth not covered by water.



Answers on page 95

# Spot the Pair: Santa's Sack

Only one of the labelled images on this page is identical to Santa's sack of presents – the rest have small differences.

Can you work out which image is an exact match?

a)

b)

c)

d)

Answers on page 95

## Missing Words: Christmas Around the Globe

Each of the sentences on the opposite page is missing a word. Can you select the one correct word or phrase from the list below to complete each of the five sentences? There is one option that does NOT fit in any of the sentences – can you work out which one it is?

**Christmas tree**

**Krampus**

**Dinner**

**Rudolph**

**Red candle**

**North Pole**

Answers on page 95

1. The tradition of decorating a ________ ________ was made popular in England by Prince Albert, Queen Victoria's husband.

2. In Ireland, a ________ ________ is lit and placed in a window offering warmth and shelter during the festive season.

3. ________, an evil accomplice to St Nicholas, roams the streets of Austria on December 5th looking for naughty children.

4. Polish families make sure they have an extra table setting for Christmas ________ in case someone turns up unannounced.

5. The first letters to Santa appeared in the USA in the nineteenth century and were often addressed to Santa living at the ________ ________.

Answers on page 95

# SOLUTIONS

## Page 5: Spot the Pair: Which Elf?

The matching image is **b**.

## Pages 6–7: Spot the Difference: Santa's Workshop

## Page 8: Festive Fun Quiz

**1.** a **2.** c **3.** b

## Page 9: How Many Presents?

There are 20 presents.

## Pages 10–11: Gift Wrapped

1 – a

2 – c

3 – e

4 – b

5 – d

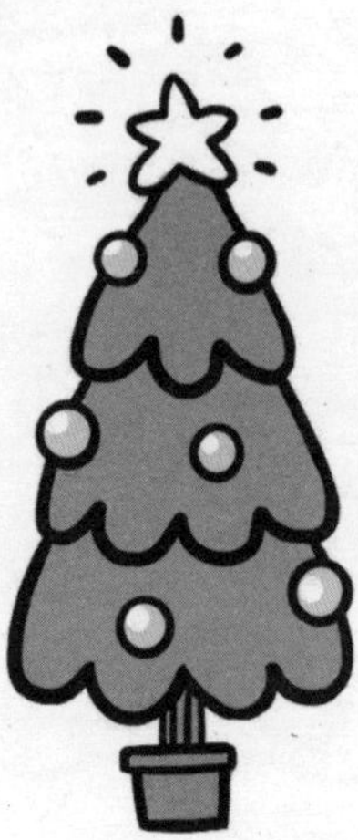

## Page 12: Christmas Traditions Quiz

**1.** b **2.** a **3.** c

## Page 13: North Pole Maze

### Page 14: Broken Bots

The pairs are: **1** and **b**, **2** and **c**, **3** and **a**.

### Page 15: Super Snowman Quiz

**1.** b
**2.** c
**3.** True
**4.** b

### Page 16: Emotion Match

**1.** d
**2.** e
**3.** b
**4.** c
**5.** a

### Page 17: Northern Delights Quiz

**1.** c. It is considered to be in international waters.
**2.** b
**3.** True

### Page 18: Christmas Riddles

**1.** In a dictionary
**2.** A Christmas tree
**3.** Snow
**4.** A sledge
**5.** A candle

## Page 19: Follow the Line: Christmas Lights Tangle

**1** with **b**, **2** with **c**, **3** with **a**, **4** with **d**

## Page 20: Hidden Words I

In the order they appear, the hidden words are:

**1.** KING (STOC<u>KING</u>)
**2.** TOE (MISTLE<u>TOE</u>)
**3.** READ (GINGERB<u>READ</u>)
**4.** IN (RE<u>IN</u>DEER)
**5.** RAT (DECO<u>RAT</u>IONS)

## Page 21: Chimney Maze

**Pages 22–23: Whose Hat?**

**1** with **b**, **2** with **f**, **3** with **a**, **4** with **e**, **5** with **c**; **d** doesn't match any elf.

**Pages 24–25: Spot the Difference: Santa's Sleigh**

## Page 26: Spot the Pair: Smiley Santa

The matching image is **c**.

## Page 27: Missing Letters: Festive Treats

In the order they appear, the words are:
MOVIE
GINGERBREAD
PRESENTS
SNOWMAN
CANES

## Pages 28–29: Missing Words: Merry Christmas

**1.** Paper
**2.** Cards
**3.** List
**4.** Decorate
**5.** Elf
**6.** Advent
**7.** Wreath

The word that is not used is **Pudding**.

## Page 30: Reorder Puzzle: Santa

The correct letter order is: **c**, **f**, **b**, **e**, **d**, **a**

## Page 31: Super Snow Quiz

**1.** b
**2.** a
**3.** True
**4.** b

## Page 32: Santa's Songs Quiz

**1.** b
**2.** c
**3.** b

## Page 33: Follow the Line: Reindeer Tangle

**1** with **c**, **2** with **b**, **3** with **a**

## Pages 34–35: Jigsaw: Sleigh Ride

The missing piece is **e.**

## Page 36: Christmas Around The World Quiz

**1.** a **2.** b **3.** c

## Page 37: Reorder Puzzle: Rudolph

The correct letter order is: **c, e, d, b, a**

## Page 38: Christmas Tree Maze

## Page 39: Christmas Garden Quiz

**1.** a **2.** b **3.** b

## Pages 40–41: Christmas Tree Shadows

1 – a
2 – c
3 – b
4 – e
5 – d

## Page 42: Snowflake Spotter

There are 15 snowflakes.

## Page 43: Missing Letters: Christmas Recipes

In the order they appear, the festive foods are:
TURKEY
MINCE PIES
CRANBERRY SAUCE
CHRISTMAS PUDDING
CHOCOLATE
CHRISTMAS CAKE
ROAST POTATOES

## Page 44: Winter Sports Quiz

**1.** c
**2.** a
**3.** True.
**4.** b

## Page 45: Missing Letters: Santa's Clothes

**1.** HAT
**2.** COAT
**3.** BELT
**4.** TROUSERS
**5.** BOOTS

## Pages 46–47: Delivery Map

**1.** Rollerskates – B5
**2.** Football – C3
**3.** Robot – E1

## Page 48: 'Tis the Season Quiz

**1.** c
**2.** b
**3.** a

## Page 49: Christmas Codebreaker

**1.** BALL
**2.** BIKE
**3.** COMPUTER
**4.** PENCIL CASE

## Page 50: Skating Fun Maze

## Page 51: Icy Trivia Quiz

**1.** b
**2.** True
**3.** b

## Pages 52–53: Spot the Difference: Snowpark Fun!

## Page 54: Christmas Foods Quiz

**1.** a **2.** c **3.** True

## Page 55: Follow the Path: Christmas Market

**1.** b – Market
**2.** d – North Pole
**3.** a – Pond
**4. c – Tree**

## Page 56: Twelve Birds of Christmas Quiz

**1.** a
**2.** b
**3.** c

## Page 57: Candy Cane Maze

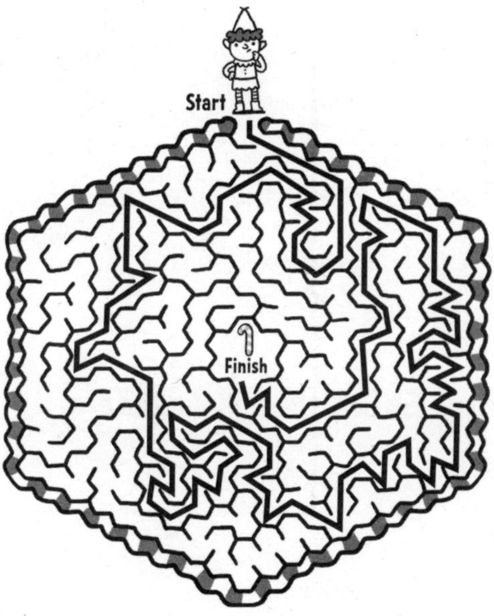

## Page 58: Spot the Pair: Gingerbread

The matching image is **c.**

a) 

b) 

d) 

## Page 59: Secret Scribbler: Decoration Time

In order, the completed words are:
TINSEL
WREATH
FAIRY
LIGHTS

## Page 60: Follow the Line: Tinsel Tangle

**1** with **b**, **2** with **a**, **3** with **c**

## Page 61: Christmas Cake Quiz

**1.** b **2.** True **3.** b

## Pages 62–63: Christmas Treasure Hunt

The instructions lead to Santa's sack. On the way, the path crosses the gingerbread man and the snowman.

## Pages 64–65: Jigsaw: Santa's Tree

The missing piece is **c**.

## Pages 66–67: Missing Words: Happy Christmas!

**1.** Cracker
**2.** Reindeer
**3.** Rudolph
**4.** Wreath
**5.** Santa
**6.** Stocking

The word that isn't used is **Elf**.

## Pages 68–69: Secret Santa

**1** with **b**, **2** with **c**, **3** with **d**, **4** with **a**

## Page 70: Secret Scribbler: Winter Wonderland

In the order they appear, the words are:

CANDY CANE
ICE SKATING
SNOWMAN
CHOCOLATE

## Page 71: Festive Riddles!

**1.** A stamp
**2.** The letter 's'
**3.** Comet
**4.** Frost

## Page 72: Hidden Words II

In the order they appear, the hidden words are:

1. ICE (SPICE)
2. KEY (DONKEY)
3. NUT (DOUGHNUT)
4. ON (SONG)
5. LAND (GARLAND)

## Page 73: Spot the Pair: Santa's Sack

The matching image is **c**.

a) 

b) 

d) 

## Pages 74–75: Missing Words: Christmas Around the Globe

1. Christmas tree
2. Red candle
3. Krampus
4. Dinner
5. North Pole

The word that isn't used is **Rudolph**.

**Look out for other books in the series!**